*The Influence of Pythagoras
on Freemasonry
and Other Essays*

By Albert G. Mackey
Manly P. Hall

Copyright © 2020 Lamp of Trismegistus. All rights reserved. No part of this publication may be reproduced or transmitted in any form or by any means, electronic or mechanical, including photocopying, recording, or by any information storage and retrieval system, without permission in writing from Lamp of Trismegistus. Reviewers may quote brief passages.

ISBN: 978-1-63118-404-8

Foundations of Freemasonry Series

Other Books in this Series and Related Titles

Masonic and Rosicrucian History by M P Hall & H Voorhis (978-1-63118-486-4)

Freemasonry, Mithraism and the Ancient Mysteries by various (978-1-63118-407-9)

The Kabbalah of Masonry & Related Writings by E Levi &c (978-1-63118-453-6)

Some Deeper Aspects of Masonic Symbolism by A E Waite (978-1-63118-461-1)

Masonic Symbolism of King Solomon's Temple by A Mackey &c (978-1-63118-442-0)

The Old Past Master by Carl H Claudy (978-1-63118-464-2)

The Mysteries of Freemasonry & the Druids by various (978-1-63118-444-4)

Rosicrucians and Speculative Masonry in the Seventeenth Century (978-1-63118-489-5)

The Two Great Pillars of Boaz and Jachin by A Mackey &c (978-1-63118-433-8)

The Regius Poem or Halliwell Manuscript by King Solomon (978-1-63118-447-5)

The Lost Keys of Freemasonry or The Secret of Hiram Abiff (978-1-63118-427-7)

Masonic Symbolism of the Apron & the Altar by various (978-1-63118-428-4)

Symbolism and Discourses on the Entered Apprentice, Fellowcraft and Master Mason Blue Lodge Degrees by various (978-1-63118-413-0)

The Legend of the Holy Grail and its Connection with Templars and Freemasons by A E Waite (978-1-63118-462-8)

American Indian Freemasonry by A C Parker (978-1-63118-460-4)

Ancient Mysteries and Secret Societies by M P Hall (978-1-63118-410-9)

The Ceremony of Initiation: Analysis & Commentary (978-1-63118-473-4)

The Master Mason's Handbook by J S M Ward (978-1-63118-474-1)

The Janeites, The Man Who Would Be King and Other Stories of Freemasonry by Rudyard Kipling (978-1-63118-480-2)

Audio Versions are also available on Audible, Amazon and Apple

Table of Contents

Introduction...7

The Influence of Pythagoras on Freemasonry
by Albert G. Mackey...9

The Golden Verses of Pythagoras...27

The Life and Philosophy of Pythagoras
by Manly P. Hall...33

INTRODUCTION

From the beginning of Modern Freemasonry's birthdate of 1717, the intelligentsia of humanity have found refuge for safe reflection within the walls of the fraternity. Masonic writers have produced a nearly incalculable amount of written musings on a multitude of esoteric and philosophical subjects, as they relate to the ancient mysteries that Freemasonry currently storehouses. Sadly, most of it appears to have sat largely unread, as American Freemasonry in particular, continues to transform itself into something that bears little resemblance to what it was originally designed to be. The true essence of Freemasonry is not that of blind patriotism or a single-minded national religion but one of Universal Brotherhood and altruism, designed for the betterment not just of its members but of society as a whole. In particular, for those who are not members of the fraternity, as Freemasonry has always acted as a beacon, to help guide humanity through darker times, with the hopes that one day we will collectively reach a truly enlightened age.

It's not uncommon for new members joining the fraternity to find little education within the walls of many modern lodges, in spite of so much written material available to the membership. Many older members are not simply uneducated with regards to real Masonic history and symbology, not to mention the vast arena of related subjects, but they are disinterested in all of it, as well.

Lamp of Trismegistus is doing its part to help preserve humanity's Masonic history by making some of these classics available to those students who are seeking to unearth the knowledge of these ancient colossi. As such, Lamp of Trismegistus offers its readers highlights of Masonic study, culled from a variety of authors and viewpoints, with the hope bringing education back into the fraternity. So, be sure to check out other titles in our *Foundations of Freemasonry Series* as well as our *Theosophical Classics, Occult Fiction, Paranormal Research Series, Esoteric Classics, Supernatural Fiction, Studies in Buddhism* and our *Christian Apocrypha Series* as well as numerous other subjects; and, don't be afraid to let a little altruism into your own heart or even into your Lodge. You can also download the audio versions of many of these titles from Audible, Amazon or Apple, for learning on the go.

THE INFLUENCE OF PYTHAGORAS ON FREEMASONRY

By Albert G. Mackey

The theory which ascribes, if not the actual origin of Freemasonry to Pythagoras, at least its introduction into Europe by him, through the school which he established at Crotona, in Italy, which was a favorite one among our early writers, may very properly be placed among the legends of the Order, since it wants all the requisites of historical authority for its support.

The notion was most probably derived from what has been called the Leland Manuscript, because it is said to have been found in the Bodleian Library, in the handwriting of that celebrated antiquary. The author of the *Life of Leland* gives this account of the manuscript:

> "*The original is said to be the handwriting of King Henry VI. and copied by Leland by order of his highness, King Henry VIII. If the authenticity of this ancient monument of literature remains unquestioned, it demands particular notice in the present publication, on account of the singularity of the subject, and no less from a due regard to the royal writer and our author, his transcriber, indefatigable in every part of literature. It will also be admitted, acknowledgment is due to the learned Mr. Locke, who, amidst the closest studies and the most strict attention to human understanding, could unbend his mind in search of this ancient treatise, which he first brought from obscurity in the year 1796.*"

This production was first brought to the attention of scholars by being published in the Gentlemen's Magazine for September, 1753, where it is stated to have been previously printed at Frankfort, in Germany, in 1748, from a copy found in "the writing- desk of a deceased brother."

The title of it, as given in the magazine, is in the following words:

> Certeyne Questyons wyth Answeres to the same, concerynge the Mystery of Maconrye; wrytenne by the hande of Kynge Henrye the Sixthe of the Name, and faythefullye copied by me Johan Leylande, Antiquarius, by the commaunde of His Highnesse.

Translated into modern speech:

> [*Certain Questions with Answers to the same, concerning the Mystery of Masonry; written by the hand of King Henry the Sixth of the Name, and faithfully copied by me, John Leland, Antiquarian, by the command of His Highness.*]

The opinion of Masonic critics of the present day is that the document is a forgery. It was most probably written about the time and in the spirit in which Chatterton composed his imitations of the Monk Rowley, and of Ireland with his impositions of Shakespeare, and was fabricated as an unsuccessful attempt to imitate the archaic language of the 15th century, and as a pious fraud intended to elevate the character and sustain the pretensions of the Masonic Fraternity by furnishing the evidence of its very ancient origin.

Such were not, however, the views of the Masonic writers of the last and beginning of the present century.

They accepted the manuscript, or rather the printed copy of it--for the original codex has never been seen--with unhesitating, faith as an authentic document. Hutchinson gave it as an appendix to his Spirit of Masonry, Preston published in the second and enlarged edition of his Illustrations, Calcott in his Candid Disquisition, Dermott in his *Ahiman Rezon,* and Krause in his *Drei Altesten Kunsturkunden.* In none of these is there the faintest hint of its being anything but an authentic document. Oliver said: "I entertain no doubt of the genuineness and authenticity of this valuable Manuscript." The same view has been entertained by Reghellini among the French, and by Krause, Fessler, and Lenning among the Germans.

Mr. Halliwell was perhaps the first of English scholars to express a doubt of its genuineness. After a long and unsuccessful search in the Bodleian Library for the original, he came, very naturally, to the conclusion that it is a forgery. Hughan and Woodford, both excellent judges, have arrived at the same conclusion, and it is now a settled question that the Leland or Locke Manuscript (for *it is known by both titles)* is a document of no historic character. It is not, however, without its value. To its appearance about the middle of the last century, and the unhesitating acceptance of its truth by the Craft at the time, we can, in all probability, assign the establishment of the doctrine that Freemasonry was of a Pythagorean origin, though it had been long before adverted to by Dr. Anderson.

Before proceeding to an examination of the rise and progress of this opinion, it will be proper to cite so much of the manuscript as connects Pythagoras with Masonry. I do not quote the whole document, though it is short, because it has so repeatedly been printed, in even elementary Masonic works, as to be readily accessible to the reader. In making my quotations I shall so far defer to the artifice of the fabricator as to preserve unchanged his poor attempt to imitate the orthography and style of the 15th century, and interpolate in brackets, when necessary, an explanation of the most unintelligible words.

The document purports to be answers by some Mason to questions proposed by King Henry VI, who, it would seem, must have taken some interest in the "Mystery of Masonry," and had sought to obtain from competent authority a knowledge of its true character.

The following are among the questions and answers:

Q. Where dyd ytt [Masonry] begynne? A. Ytt dyd begynne with the fyrst menne, yn the Este, which were before the fyrste Manne of the Weste, and comyngc westlye, ytt hathe broughte herwyth alle comfortes to the wylde and comfortlesse.

Translated into modern speech:

[Question: *Where did Masonry begin? Answer: It did begin with the first men in the East, which were before the first man of the West, and coming West, it hath brought herewith all comforts to the wild and comfortless.*]

Q. Who dyd brynge ytt Westye ? A. The Venetians [Phoenicians] who beynge grate Merchandes comed ffyrst ffrome the Este yn Venctia [Phoenicia] for the commodyte of Merchaundysinge beithe [both] Este and Weste bey the redde and Myddlelonde [Mediterranean] Sees.

Translated into modern speech:

[Question: *Who did bring it West? Answer: The Phoenicians, who being great merchants come first from the East in Phoenicia for the commodity of merchandizing both East and West by the Red and Mediterranean Seas.*]

Q. Howe comede ytt yn Englonde? A. Peter Gower [Pythagoras] a Grecian journeyedde tor kunnynge yn Egypt and in Syria and in everyche Londe whereat the Venetians [Phoenicians] hadde plauntedde Maconrye and wynnynge Entraunce yn all Lodges of Maconnes, he lerned muche, and retournedde and woned [dwelt] yn Cirecia Magna wachsynge [growing] and becommynge a myghtye wyseacre [philosopher] and gratelyche renouned and here he framed a grate Lodge at Groton [Crotona] and maked many Maconnes, some whereoffe dyd journeye yn Fraunce, and maked manye Maconnes wherefromme, yn processe of Tyme, the Arte passed yn Engelonde."

Translated into modern speech:

[Question: *How came it in England? Answer: Peter Gower (Pythagoras), a Grecian, journeyed for knowledge in Egypt and in*

Syria and in every other land where the Phoenicians had planted Masonry and winning entrance in all Lodges of Masons, he learned much, and returned and dwelt in Cirecia Magna (Southern Italy), growing and becoming a mighty philosopher and greatly renowned and here he formed a great Lodge at Crotona and made many Masons, some whereof did journey in France, and made many Masons wherefrom, in process of time, the Art passed in England.]

I am convinced that there was a French original of this document, from which language the fabricator translated it into archaic English. The internal proofs of this are to be found in the numerous preservations of French idioms. Thus we meet with Peter Gower, evidently derived from Pythagore, pronounced Petagore, the French for Pythagoras; Maconrye and Maconnes, for Masonry and Masons, the French c in the word being used instead of the English s,- the phrase wynnynge the Facultye of Abrac, which is a pure Gallic idiom, instead of acquiring the faculty, the word gayner being indifferently used in French as signifying to win or to acquire,- the word Freres for Brethren,- and the statement, in the spirit of French nationality, that Masonry was brought into England out of France.

None of these idiomatic phrases or national peculiarities would have been likely to occur if the manuscript had been originally written by an Englishman and in the English language. But be this as it may, the document had no sooner appeared than it seemed to inspire contemporary Masonic writers with the idea that Masonry and the school of Pythagoras, which he established at Crotona, in Italy, about five centuries before Christ, were closely connected-an idea which was very generally adopted by their successors, so that it came at last to be a point of the orthodox Masonic creed.

Thus Preston, in his Illustrations of Masonry, when commenting on the dialogue contained in this document, says that, "the records of the fraternity inform us that Pythagoras was regularly initiated into Masonry; and being properly instructed in the mysteries of the Art, he was much improved, and propagated the principles of the Order in other countries into which he afterwards travelled."

Calcott, in his Candid Disquisition, speaks of the Leland Manuscript as "an antique relation, from whence may be gathered many of the original principles of the ancient society, on which the institution of Freemasonry was ingrafted" by the "ancient society meaning the school of Pythagoras."

Hutchinson, in his Spirit of Masonry, quotes this "ancient Masonic record," as he calls it, and says that "it brings us positive evidence of the Pythagorean doctrine and Basilidean principles making the foundation of our religious and moral duties." Two of the lectures in his work are appropriated to a discussion of the doctrines of Pythagoras in connection with the Masonic system. But this theory of the Pythagorean origin of Freemasonry does not owe its existence to the writers of the middle of the 18th century.

This theory had been advanced at an early period and soon after the Revival in 1717, by Dr. Anderson. In the first edition of the Constitutions, published in 1723, he alludes to Pythagoras as having borrowed great knowledge from the Chaldean Magi and the Babylonish Jews, but he is more explicit in his *Defense of Masonry,* published in 1730, wherein he says: "I am fully convinced that Freemasonry is very nearly allied to the old Pythagorean Discipline, from whence, I am persuaded, it may in some circumstances very justly claim a descent."

Now, how are we to explain the way in which this tradition of the connection of the Philosopher of Samos first acquired a place among the legends of the Craft? The solution of the problem does not appear to be very difficult.

In none of the old manuscript constitutions which contain what has been called the Legend of the Guild, or the Legend of the Craft, is there, with a single exception, any allusion to the name of Pythagoras. That exception is found in the Cooke Manuscript of 1450, where the legendist, after relating the story of the two pillars inscribed with all the sciences, which had been erected by Jabal before the Flood, adds, in lines 318-326, this statement:

> "And after this flode many yeres as the cronyclc tellcth these ii were founde and as the polycronicon seyeth that a grete clerke that called putogaras [Pythagoras] fonde that one and hermes the philisophre fonde that other, and thei tought forthe the sciens that thei fonde therein ywritten."

Translated into modern speech:

> [*And after this flood, many years as the chronicle telleth, these 2 were found and as the Polychronicon sayeth, that a great clerk, that called Pythagoras, found that one, and Hermes the philosopher*

found that other, and they taught forth the sciences that they found therein written.]

Now, although the Cooke Manuscript is the earliest of the old records, after the Halliwell Manuscript of 1390 (a.k.a. *The Regius Poem),* none of the subsequent constitutions have followed it in this allusion to Pythagoras. This was because the writer of the Cooke Manuscript, being in possession of the *Polychronicon* of the monk Ranulf Higden, an edition of which had been printed during his time by William Caxton, he had liberally borrowed from that historical work and incorporated parts of it into his Legend. Of these interpolations, the story of the finding of one of the pillars by Pythagoras is one. The writer acknowledges his indebtedness for the statement to Higden's *Polychronicon.* But it formed no part of the Legend of the Craft, and hence no notice is taken of it in the subsequent manuscript copies of the Legend. In none of them is Pythagoras even named.

It is evident, then, that in the 14th and following centuries, to the beginning of the 18th, the theory of the Pythagorean origin of Freemasonry, or of the connection of the Grecian philosopher with it, was not recognized by the Craft as any part of the traditional history of the Fraternity. There is no safer rule than that of the old schoolmen, which teaches us that we must reason alike concerning that which does not appear and that which does not exist-"de non apparentibus et de non existentibus, eadem est ratio." The old craftsmen who fabricated the Legend were workmen and not scholars; they were neither acquainted with the scholastic nor the ancient philosophy; they said nothing about Pythagoras because they knew nothing about him.

But about the beginning of the 18th century a change took place, not only in the organization of the Masonic institution, but also in the character and qualifications of the men who were engaged in producing the modification, or we might more properly call it the revolution.

Although in the 17th, and perhaps in the 16th century, many persons were admitted into the Lodges of Operative Masons who were not professional builders, it is, I think, evident that the society did not assume a purely speculative form until the year 1717. The Revival in that year, by the election of Anthony Sayer, "Gentleman," as Grand Master; Jacob Lamball, a "Carpenter," and Joseph Elliott, a "Captain," as Grand Wardens, proves that the control of the society was to be taken out of the hands of the Operative Masons.

Among those who were at about that time engaged in the reconstruction of the Institution were James Anderson and Theophilus Desaguliers. Anderson was a Master of Arts, and afterward a Doctor of Divinity, the minister of a church in London, and an author; Desaguliers was a Doctor of Laws, a fellow of the Royal Society, and a teacher of Experimental Philosophy of no little reputation. Both of these men, as scholars, were thoroughly conversant with the system of Pythagoras, and they were not unwilling to take advantage of his symbolic method of inculcating his doctrine, and to introduce some of his symbols into the symbolism of the Order, which they were renovating.

Iamblichus, the biographer of Pythagoras, tells us that while the sage was on his travels he caused himself to be initiated into all the mysteries of Byblos and Tyre and those which were practiced in many parts of Syria. But as these mysteries were originally received by the Phoenicians from Egypt, he passed over into that country, where he remained twenty-two years, occupying himself in the study of geometry, astronomy, and all the initiations of the gods, until he was carried a captive into Babylon by the soldiers of Cambyses. There he freely associated with the Magi in their religion; and their studies, and, having obtained a thorough knowledge of music, the science of numbers, and other arts, he finally returned to Greece.

The school of philosophy which Pythagoras afterward established at the city of Crotona, in Italy, differed from those of all the other philosophers of Greece, in the austerities of initiation to which his disciples were subject in the degrees of probation into which they were divided, and in the method which he adopted of veiling his instructions under symbolic forms. In his various travels he had imbibed the mystical notions prevalent among the Egyptians and the Chaldeans, and had borrowed some of their modes of initiation into their religious mysteries, which he adopted in the method by which he communicated his own principles.

George Grote, in his *History of Greece*, has very justly said that "Pythagoras represents in part the scientific tendencies of his age, in part also the spirit of mysticism and of special fraternities for religious and ascetic observance which became diffused throughout Greece in the 6th century before the

Christian era." Of the character of the philosophy of Pythagoras and of his method of instruction, which certainly bore a very close resemblance to that adopted by the founders of the speculative system, such cultivated scholars as Anderson and Desaguliers certainly were not ignorant. And if, among those who were engaged with them in the construction of this new and improved school of speculative Masonry, there were any whose limited scholastic attainments would not enable them to consult the Greek biographies of Pythagoras by Iamblichus and by Porphyry, they had at hand and readily accessible an English translation of M. Dacier's life of the philosopher, containing also an elaborate explication of his symbols, together with a translation of the Commentaries of Herodes on the Golden Verses of Pythagoras, all embraced in one volume and published in London in the year 1707, by the celebrated bibliopole Jacob Tonson.

There was abundant material and ready opportunity for the partially unlearned as well as for the more erudite to obtain a familiarity with the philosophy of Pythagoras, his method of initiation, and his system of symbols.

It is not, therefore, surprising that these "Revivalists," as they have been called, should have delighted, as Anderson has done in his *Defense of Masonry,* to compare the two schools of the Pythagoreans and the Freemasons; that they should have dwelt on their great similarity; and in the development of their speculative system should have adopted many symbols from the former which do not appear to have been known to or used by the old Operative Masons whom they succeeded.

Among the first Pythagorean symbols which were adopted by the Speculative Masons was the symbolism of the science of numbers, which appears in the earliest rituals extant, and of which Dr. Oliver has justly said, in his posthumous work entitled The Pythagorean Triangle, that "the Pythagoreans had so high an opinion of it that they considered it to be the origin of all things, and thought a knowledge of it to be equivalent to a knowledge of God."

This symbolism of numbers, which was adopted into Speculative Masonry at a very early period after the Revival, has been developed and enlarged in successive revisions of the lectures, until at the present day it constitutes one of the most important and curious parts of the system of Freemasonry. But we have no evidence that the same system of numerical symbolism, having the Pythagorean and modern Masonic interpretation, prevailed among the Craft anterior to the beginning of the 18th century.

It was the work of the Revivalists, who, as scholars familiar with the mystical philosophy of Pythagoras, deemed it expedient to introduce it into the equally mystical philosophy of Speculative Masonry. In fact, the Traveling Freemasons, Builders, or Operative Masons of the Middle Ages, who were the real predecessors of the Speculative Masons of the 18th century, did not, so far as we can learn from their remains, practice any of the symbolism of Pythagoras. Their symbol, such as the vesica pisces, the cross, the rose, or certain mathematical figures, were derived either from the legends of the church or from the principles of geometry applied to the art of building. These skillful architects who, in the dark ages, when few men could read or write, erected edifices surpassing the works of ancient Greece or Rome, and which have never been equaled by modern builders, were wonderful in their peculiar skill, but were wholly ignorant of metaphysics or philosophy, and borrowed nothing from Pythagoras.

Between the period of the Revival and the adoption of the Prestonian system, in 1772, the lectures of Freemasonry underwent at least seven revisions. In each of these, the fabricators of which were such cultivated scholars as Dr. Desaguliers, Martin Clare, a President of the Royal Society, Thomas Dunckerley, a man of considerable literary attainments, and others of like character, there was a gradual increment of Pythagorean symbols. Among these, one of the most noted is the forty-seventh proposition of Euclid, which is said to have been discovered by Pythagoras, and which the introducer of it into the Masonic system, in his explanation of the symbol, claims the sage to have been "an ancient brother."

For some time after the Revival, the symbols of Pythagoras, growing into gradual use among the Craft, were referred to simply as an evidence of the great similarity which existed between the two systems-a theory which, so far as it respects modern Speculative Masonry, may be accepted with but little hesitation.

The most liberal belief on this subject was that the two systems were nearly allied, but, except in the modified statement of Anderson, already quoted from his *Defense of Masonry,* there was no claim in the years immediately succeeding the Revival that the one was in direct descent from the other.

In none of the speeches, lectures, or essays of the early part of the last century, which have been preserved, is there any allusion to this as a received theory of the Craft.

Drake, in his speech before the Grand Lodge of York, delivered in 1726 does indeed, speak of Pythagoras, not as the founder of Masonry, but only in connection with Euclid and Archimedes as great proficients in Geometry, whose works have been the basis "on which the learned have built at different times so many noble superstructures." And of Geometry, he calls it "that noble and useful science which must have begun and goes hand in hand with Masonry," an assertion which, to use the old chorus of the Masons, nobody will deny.

But to say that Geometry is closely connected with Operative Masonry, and that Pythagoras was a great geometrician, is very different from saying that he was a Mason and propagated Masonry in Europe.

Martin Clare, in his lecture on the Advantages Enjoyed by the Fraternity, whose date is 1735, does not even mention the name of Pythagoras, although, in one passage at least, when referring to "those great and worthy spirits with whom we are intimately related," he had a fair opportunity to refer to that illustrious sage.

In a *Discourse Upon Masonry*, delivered before a Lodge of England in 1742, now lying before me, in which the origin of the Order is fully discussed, there is not one word of reference to Pythagoras. The same silence is preserved in a Lecture on the Connection Between Freemasonry and Religion, by the Rev. C. Brockwell, published in 1747.

But after the middle of the century the frequent references in the lectures to the Pythagorean symbols, and especially to that important one, in its Masonic as well as its geometrical value, the forty-seventh proposition, began to lead the members of the society to give to Pythagoras the credit of a relationship to the order to which historically he had no claim.

Thus, in *A Search After Truth,* delivered in the Lodge in 1752, the author says that "Solon, Plato, and Pythagoras, and from them the Grecian literati in general in a great measure, were obliged for their learning to Masonry and the labors of some of our ancient brethren."

And then, when this notion of the Pythagorean origin of Freemasonry began to take root in the minds of the Craft, it was more firmly established by the appearance in 1753, in the Gentleman's Magazine, of that spurious document already quoted, in which, by a "pious fraud," the fabricator of it sought to give the form of an historical record to the statement that Pythagoras, learning his Masonry of the Eastern Magi had brought it to Italy and established a Lodge at Crotona, whence the institution was propagated throughout Europe, and from France into England.

As to this statement in the Leland MS., it may be sufficient to say that the sect of Pythagoras did not subsist longer than to the end of the reign of Alexander the Great. So far from disseminating its Lodges or schools after the Christian era, we may cite the authority of the learned Dacier, who says that "in after ages there were here and there some disciples of Pythagoras, but these were only private persons who never established any society, nor had the Pythagoreans any longer a public school."

And so the result of this investigation into the theory of the Pythagorean origin of Freemasonry may be briefly epitomized thus: The mediaeval Freemasons never entertained any such theory, nor in their architectural labors did they adopt any of his symbols. The writer of the Cooke MS., in 1490, having at hand Higden's Polychronicon, in Trevisa's translation, a new edition of which had just been printed by Caxton, incorporated into the Legend of the Craft some of the historical statements (such *as they were*) of the Monk of Chester, but they were extraneous to and formed no part of the original Legend. Therefore, in all the subsequent Old Records these interpolations were rejected and the Legend of the Craft, as accepted by the writers of the manuscripts which succeeded that of the Cooke codex, from 1550 to 1701, contained no mention of Pythagoras.

Upon the Revival, in 1717, which was really the beginning of genuine Speculative Masonry, the scholars who fabricated the scheme, finding the symbolic teaching of Pythagoras very apposite, adopted some of its symbols, especially those relating to numbers in the new Speculative system, which they were forming.

By the continued additions of subsequent ritualists these symbols were greatly increased, so that the name and the philosophy of Pythagoras became familiar to the Craft, and finally, in 1753, a forged document was published which claimed him as the founder and propagator of Masonry.

In later days this theory has continued to be maintained by a few writers, and the received rituals of the Order require it as a part of the orthodox Masonic creed, that Pythagoras was a Mason and an ancient brother and patron of the Order.

And, while neither early Masonic tradition nor any historical records exist which support such a belief, Pythagoras has since become an important symbol of our esteemed Order.

THE GOLDEN VERSES OF PYTHAGORAS

Attributed to Pythagoras

1. First worship the Immortal Gods, as they are established and ordained by the Law.

2. Reverence the Oath, and next the Heroes, full of goodness and light.

3. Honor likewise the Terrestrial Dæmons by rendering them the worship lawfully due to them.

4. Honor likewise thy parents, and those most nearly related to thee.

5. Of all the rest of mankind, make him thy friend who distinguishes himself by his virtue.

6. Always give ear to his mild exhortations, and take example from his virtuous and useful actions.

7. Avoid as much as possible hating thy friend for a slight fault.

8. And understand that power is a near neighbor to necessity.

9. Know that all these things are as I have told thee; and accustom thyself to overcome and vanquish these passions:

10. First gluttony, sloth, sensuality, and anger.

11. Do nothing evil, neither in the presence of others, nor privately;

12. But above all things respect thyself.

13. In the next place, observe justice in thy actions and in thy words.

14. And accustom not thyself to behave thyself in any thing without rule, and without reason.

15. But always make this reflection, that it is ordained by destiny that all men shall die.

16. And that the goods of fortune are uncertain; and that as they may be acquired, so may they likewise be lost.

17. Concerning all the calamities that men suffer by divine fortune,

18. Support with patience thy lot, be it what it may, and never repine at it.

19. But endeavor what thou canst to remedy it.

20. And consider that fate does not send the greatest portion of these misfortunes to good men.

21. There are among men many sorts of reasonings, good and bad;

22. Admire them not too easily, nor reject them.

23. But if falsehoods be advanced, hear them with mildness, and arm thyself with patience.

24. Observe well, on every occasion, what I am going to tell thee:

25. Let no man either by his words, or by his deeds, ever seduce thee.

26. Nor entice thee to say or to do what is not profitable for thyself.

27. Consult and deliberate before thou act, that thou mayest not commit foolish actions.

28. For it is the part of a miserable man to speak and to act without reflection.

29. But do that which will not afflict thee afterwards, nor oblige thee to repentance.

30. Never do anything which thou dost not understand.

31. But learn all thou ought'st to know, and by that means thou wilt lead a very pleasant life.

32. In no wise neglect the health of thy body;

33. But give it drink and meat in due measure, and also the exercise of which it has need.

34. Now by measure I mean what will not incommode thee.

35. Accustom thyself to a way of living that is neat and decent without luxury.

36. Avoid all things that will occasion envy.

37. And be not prodigal out of season, like one who knows not what is decent and honorable.

38. Neither be covetous nor miserly; a due measure is excellent in these things.

39. Do only the things that cannot hurt thee, and deliberate before thou dost them.

40. Never suffer sleep to close thy eyelids, after thy going to bed,

41. Till thou hast examined by thy reason all thy actions of the day.

42. Wherein have I done amiss? What have I done? What have I omitted that I ought to have done?

43. If in this examination thou find that thou hast done amiss, reprimand thyself severely for it;

44. And if thou hast done any good, rejoice.

45. Practice thoroughly all these things; meditate on them well; thou oughtest to love them with all thy heart.

46. 'Tis they that will put thee in the way of divine virtue.

47. I swear it by him who has transmitted into our souls the Sacred Quaternion, the source of nature, whose cause is eternal.

48. But never begin to set thy hand to any work, till thou hast first prayed to the gods to accomplish what thou art going to begin.

49. When thou hast made this habit familiar to thee,

50. Thou wilt know the constitution of the Immortal Gods and of men.

51. Even how far the different beings extend, and what contains and binds them together.

52. Thou shalt likewise know that according to Law, the nature of this universe is in all things alike,

53. So that thou shalt not hope what thou ought'st not to hope; and nothing in this world shall be hid from thee.

54. Thou wilt likewise know, that men draw upon themselves their own misfortunes voluntarily, and of their own free choice.

55. Unhappy that they are! They neither see nor understand that their good is near them.

56. Few know how to deliver themselves out of their misfortunes.

57. Such is the fate that blinds mankind, and takes away his senses.

58. Like huge cylinders they roll to and fro, and always oppressed with ills innumerable.

59. For fatal strife, innate, pursues them everywhere, tossing them up and down; nor do they perceive it.

60. Instead of provoking and stirring it up, they ought, by yielding, to avoid it.

61. Oh! Jupiter, our Father! if Thou would'st deliver men from all the evils that oppress them,

62. Show them of what dæmon they make use. 63. But take courage; the race of man is divine.

64. Sacred nature reveals to them the most hidden mysteries.

65. If she impart to thee her secrets, thou wilt easily perform all the things which I have ordained thee.

66. And by the healing of thy soul, thou wilt deliver it from all evils, from all afflictions.

67. But abstain thou from the meats, which we have forbidden in the purifications and in the deliverance of the soul;

68. Make a just distinction of them, and examine all things well.

69. Leaving thyself always to be guided and directed by the understanding that comes from above, and that ought to hold the reins.

70. And when, after having divested thyself of thy mortal body, thou arrivest at the most pure Æther,

71. Thou shalt be a God, immortal, incorruptible, and Death shall have no more dominion over thee.

THE LIFE AND PHILOSOPHY OF PYTHAGORAS

By Manly P. Hall

PART I

While Mnesarchus, the father of Pythagoras, was in the city of Delphi on matters pertaining to his business as a merchant, he and his wife, Parthenis, decided to consult the oracle of Delphi as to whether the Fates were favorable for their return voyage to Syria. When the Pythoness (prophetess of Apollo) seated herself on the golden tripod over the yawning vent of the oracle, she did not answer the question they had asked, but told Mnesarchus that his wife was then with child and would give birth to a son who was destined to surpass all men in beauty and wisdom, and who throughout the course of his life would contribute much to the benefit of mankind. Mnesarchus was so deeply impressed by the prophecy that he changed his wife's name to Pythasis, in honor of the Pythian priestess. When the child was born at Sidon in Phœnicia, it was- -as the oracle had said--a son. Mnesarchus and Pythasis named the child Pythagoras, for they believed that he had been predestined by the oracle.

Many strange legends have been preserved concerning the birth of Pythagoras. Some maintained that he was no mortal man: that he was one of the gods who had taken a human body to enable him to come into the world and instruct the human race. Pythagoras was one of the many sages and saviors of antiquity for whom an immaculate conception is asserted. In his *Anacalypsis,* Godfrey Higgins writes: "The first striking circumstance in which the history of Pythagoras agrees with the history of Jesus is, that they were natives of nearly the same country; the former being born at Sidon, the latter at Bethlehem, both in Syria. The father of Pythagoras, as well as the father of Jesus, was prophetically informed that his wife should bring forth a son, who should be a benefactor to mankind. They were both born when their mothers were from home on journeys, Joseph and his wife having gone up to Bethlehem to be taxed, and the father of Pythagoras having travelled from Samos, his residence, to Sidon, about his mercantile concerns. Pythais [Pythasis], the mother of Pythagoras, had a connection with an Apolloniacal specter, or ghost, of the God Apollo, or God Sol, (of course this must have been a *holy* ghost, and here we have the Holy Ghost) which afterward appeared to her husband, and told him that he must have no connection with his wife during her pregnancy--a story evidently the same as that relating to Joseph and Mary. From these peculiar circumstances, Pythagoras was known by the same title as Jesus, namely, the *son of God;* and was supposed by the multitude to be under the influence of Divine inspiration."

This most famous philosopher was born sometime between 600 and 590 B.C., and the length of his life has been estimated at nearly one hundred years.

The teachings of Pythagoras indicate that he was thoroughly conversant with the precepts of Oriental and Occidental esotericism. He traveled among the Jews and was instructed by the Rabbis concerning the secret traditions of Moses, the lawgiver of Israel. Later the School of the Essenes was conducted chiefly for the purpose of interpreting the Pythagorean symbols. Pythagoras was initiated into the Egyptian, Babylonian, and Chaldean Mysteries. Although it is believed by some that he was a disciple of Zoroaster, it is doubtful whether his instructor of that name was the God-man now revered by the Parsees. While accounts of his travels differ, historians agree that he visited many countries and studied at the feet of many masters.

"After having acquired all which it was possible for him to learn of the Greek philosophers and, presumably, become an initiate in the Eleusinian mysteries, he went to Egypt, and after many rebuffs and refusals, finally succeeded in securing initiation in the Mysteries of Isis, at the hands of the priests of Thebes. Then this intrepid 'joiner' wended his way into Phoenicia and Syria where the Mysteries of Adonis were conferred upon him, and crossing to the valley of the Euphrates he tarried long enough to become versed in, the secret lore of the Chaldeans, who still dwelt in the vicinity of Babylon. Finally, he made his greatest and most historic venture through Media and Persia into Hindustan where he remained several years as a pupil and initiate of the learned Brahmins of Elephanta and Ellora." (See *Ancient Freemasonry*, by Frank C. Higgins) The same author adds that the name of Pythagoras is still preserved in the records of the Brahmins as *Yavancharya*, the Ionian Teacher.

Pythagoras was said to have been the first man to call himself a *philosopher;* in fact, the world is indebted to him for the word *philosopher.* Before that time the wise men had called themselves *sages,* which was interpreted to mean *those who know.* Pythagoras was more modest. He coined the word *philosopher,* which he defined as *one who is attempting to find out.*

After returning from his wanderings, Pythagoras established a school, or as it has been sometimes called, a university, at Crotona, a Dorian colony in Southern Italy. Upon his arrival at Crotona he was regarded askance, but after a short time those holding important positions in the surrounding colonies sought his counsel in matters of great moment. He gathered around him a small group of sincere disciples whom he instructed in the secret wisdom which had been revealed to him, and also in the fundamentals of occult mathematics, music, and astronomy, which he considered to be the triangular foundation of all the arts and sciences.

When he was about sixty years old, Pythagoras married one of his disciples, and seven children resulted from the union. His wife was a remarkably able woman, who not only inspired him during the years of his life but after his assassination continued to promulgate his doctrines.

As is so often the case with genius, Pythagoras by his outspokenness incurred both political and personal enmity. Among those who came for initiation was one who, because Pythagoras refused to admit him, determined to destroy both the man and his philosophy. By means of false propaganda, this disgruntled one turned the minds of the common people against the philosopher. Without warning, a band of murderers descended upon the little group of buildings where the great teacher and his disciples dwelt, burned the structures and killed Pythagoras.

Accounts of the philosopher's death do not agree. Some say that he was murdered with his disciples; others that, on escaping from Crotona with a small band of followers, he was trapped and burned alive by his enemies in a little house where the band had decided to rest for the night. Another account

PYTHAGORAS, THE FIRST PHILOSOPHER[1]

---

[1] During his youth, Pythagoras was a disciple of Pherecydes and Hermodamas, and while in his teens became renowned for the clarity of his philosophic concepts. In height he exceeded six feet; his body was as perfectly formed as that of Apollo. Pythagoras was the personification of majesty and power, and in his presence a felt humble and afraid. As he grew older, his physical power increased rather than waned, so that as he approached the century mark he was actually in the prime of life. The influence of this great soul over those about him was such that a word of praise from Pythagoras filled his disciples with ecstasy,

states that, finding themselves trapped in the burning structure, the disciples threw themselves into the flames, making of their own bodies a bridge over which Pythagoras escaped, only to die of a broken heart a short time afterwards as the result of grieving over the apparent fruitlessness of his efforts to serve and illuminate mankind.

His surviving disciples attempted to perpetuate his doctrines, but they were persecuted on every hand and very little remains today as a testimonial to the greatness of this philosopher. It is said that the disciples of Pythagoras never addressed him or referred to him by his own name, but always as *The Master* or *That Man. This may have been because of the fact that the name Pythagoras was believed to consist of a certain number of specially arranged letters with great sacred significance. The Word* magazine has printed an article by T. R. Prater, showing that Pythagoras initiated his candidates by means of a certain formula concealed within the letters of his own name. This may explain why the word Pythagoras was so highly revered.

After the death of Pythagoras his school gradually disintegrated, but those who had benefited by its teachings revered the memory of the great philosopher, as during his life they had reverenced the man himself. As time went on, Pythagoras came to be regarded as a god rather than a man, and his scattered disciples were bound together by their common admiration for the transcendent genius of their teacher. Edouard Schure, in his *Pythagoras and the Delphic Mysteries,* relates

---

while one committed suicide because the Master became momentarily irritate over something he had dome. Pythagoras was so impressed by this tragedy that he never again spoke unkindly to or about anyone.

the following incident as illustrative of the bond of fellowship uniting the members of the Pythagorean School:

> "One of them who had fallen upon sickness and poverty was kindly taken in by an innkeeper. Before dying he traced a few mysterious signs (the pentagram, no doubt) on the door of the inn and said to the host, 'Do not be uneasy, one of my brothers will pay my debts.' A year afterwards, as a stranger was passing by this inn he saw the signs and said to the host, 'I am a Pythagorean; one of my brothers died here; tell me what I owe you on his account.'"

Frank C. Higgins, gives an excellent compendium of the Pythagorean tenets in the following outline:

> "Pythagoras' teachings are of the most transcendental importance to Masons, inasmuch as they are the necessary fruit of his contact with the leading philosophers of the whole civilized world of his own day, and must represent that in which all were agreed, shorn of all weeds of controversy. Thus, the determined stand made by Pythagoras, in defense of pure monotheism, is sufficient evidence that the tradition to the effect that the unity of God was the supreme secret of all the ancient initiations is substantially correct. The philosophical school of Pythagoras was, in a measure, also a series of initiations, for he caused his pupils to pass through a series of degrees and never permitted them personal contact with himself until they had reached the higher grades. According to his biographers, his degrees

were three in number. The first, that of 'Mathematicus,' assuring his pupils proficiency in mathematics and geometry, which was then, as it would be now if Masonry were properly inculcated, the basis upon which all other knowledge was erected. Secondly, the degree of 'Theoreticus,' which dealt with superficial applications of the exact sciences, and, lastly, the degree of 'Electus,' which entitled the candidate to pass forward into the light of the fullest illumination which he was capable of absorbing. The pupils of the Pythagorean school were divided into 'exoterici,' or pupils in the outer grades, and 'esoterici,' after they had passed the third degree of initiation and were entitled to the secret wisdom. Silence, secrecy and unconditional obedience were cardinal principles of this great order."

PART II:

PYTHAGORIC FUNDAMENTALS

The study of geometry, music, and astronomy was considered essential to a rational understanding of God, man, or Nature, and no one could accompany Pythagoras as a disciple who was not thoroughly familiar with these sciences. Many came seeking admission to his school. Each applicant was tested on these three subjects, and if found ignorant, was summarily dismissed.

Pythagoras was not an extremist. He taught moderation in all things rather than excess in anything, for he believed that an excess of virtue was in itself a vice. One of his favorite statements was: "We must avoid with our utmost endeavor, and amputate with fire and sword, and by all other means, from the body, sickness; from the soul, ignorance; from the belly, luxury; from a city, sedition; from a family, discord; and from all things, excess." Pythagoras also believed that there was no crime equal to that of anarchy.

All men know what they *want*, but few know what they *need*. Pythagoras warned his disciples that when they prayed they should not pray for themselves; that when they asked things of the gods they should not ask things for themselves, because no man knows what is good for him and it is for this reason undesirable to ask for things which, if obtained, would only prove to be injurious.

The God of Pythagoras was the *Monad*, or the One that is Everything. He described God as the Supreme Mind distributed throughout all parts of the universe--the Cause of all things, the Intelligence of all things, and the Power within all things. He further declared the motion of God to be circular, the body of God to be composed of the substance of light, and the nature of God to be composed of the substance of truth.

Pythagoras declared that the eating of meat clouded the reasoning faculties. While he did not condemn its use or totally abstain therefrom himself, he declared that judges should refrain from eating meat before a trial, in order that those who appeared before them might receive the most honest and astute decisions. When Pythagoras decided (as he often did) to retire into the temple of God for an extended period of time to meditate and pray, he took with his supply of specially prepared food and drink. The food consisted of equal parts of the seeds of poppy and sesame, the skin of the sea onion from which the juice had been thoroughly extracted, the flower of daffodil, the leaves of mallows, and a paste of barley and peas. These he compounded together with the addition of wild honey. For a beverage he took the seeds of cucumbers, dried raisins (with seeds removed), the flowers of coriander, the seeds of mallows and purslane, scraped cheese, meal, and cream, mixed together and sweetened with wild honey. Pythagoras claimed that this was the diet of Hercules while wandering in the Libyan desert and was according to the formula given to that hero by the goddess Ceres herself.

The favorite method of healing among the Pythagoreans was by the aid of poultices. These people also knew the magic properties of vast numbers of plants. Pythagoras highly esteemed the medicinal properties of the sea onion, and he is said to have written an entire volume on the subject. Such a work, however, is not known at the present time. Pythagoras discovered that music had great therapeutic power and he prepared special harmonies for various diseases. He apparently experimented also with color, attaining considerable success. One of his unique curative processes resulted from his discovery of the healing value of certain verses from the *Odyssey* and the *Iliad* of Homer. These he caused to be read to persons suffering from certain ailments. He was opposed to surgery in all its forms and also objected to cauterizing. He would not permit the disfigurement of the human body, for such, in his estimation, was a sacrilege against the dwelling place of the gods.

Pythagoras taught that friendship was the truest and nearest perfect of all relationships. He declared that in Nature there was a friendship of all for all; of gods for men; of doctrines one for another; of the soul for the body; of the rational part for the irrational part; of philosophy for its theory; of men for one another; of countrymen for one another; that friendship also existed between strangers, between a man and his wife, his children, and his servants. All bonds without friendship were shackles, and there was no virtue in their maintenance. Pythagoras believed that relationships were essentially mental rather than physical, and that a stranger of sympathetic intellect was closer to him than a blood relation whose viewpoint was at variance with his own. Pythagoras defined knowledge as the fruitage of mental accumulation. He believed that it would be obtained in many ways, but principally through observation. Wisdom was the understanding of the source or cause of all things, and this could be secured only by raising the intellect to a point where it intuitively cognized the invisible manifesting outwardly through the visible, and thus became capable of bringing itself *en rapport* with the spirit of things rather than with their forms. The ultimate source that wisdom could cognize was the *Monad,* the mysterious permanent atom of the Pythagoreans.

Pythagoras taught that both man and the universe were made in the image of God; that both being made in the same image, the understanding of one predicated the knowledge of the other. He further taught that there was a constant interplay between the Grand Man (the universe) and man (the little universe).

Pythagoras believed that all the sidereal bodies were alive and that the forms of the planets and stars were merely bodies encasing souls, minds, and spirits in the same manner that the visible human form is but the encasing vehicle for an invisible spiritual organism which is, in reality, the conscious individual. Pythagoras regarded the planets as magnificent deities, worthy of the adoration and respect of man. All these deities, however, he considered subservient to the One First Cause within whom they all existed temporarily, as mortality exists in the midst of immortality.

The famous Pythagorean letter "Y" signified the power of choice and was used in the Mysteries as emblematic of the

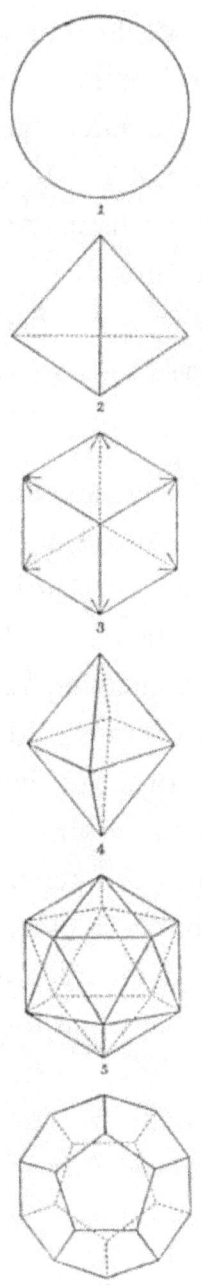

[2] Forking of the Ways. The central stem separated into two parts, one branching to the right and the other to the left. The branch to the right was called *Divine Wisdom* and the one to the left *Earthly Wisdom*. Youth, personified by the candidate, walking the Path of Life, symbolized by the central stem of the "Y", reaches the point where the Path divides. The neophyte must then choose whether he will take the left-hand path and, following the dictates of his lower nature, enter upon a span of folly and thoughtlessness which will inevitably result in his undoing, or whether he will take the right-hand road and through integrity, industry, and sincerity ultimately regain union with the immortals in the superior spheres.

It is probable that Pythagoras obtained his concept of the "Y" from the Egyptians, who included in certain of their initiatory rituals a scene in which the candidate was confronted by two female figures.

---

[2] Depiction of THE SYMMETRICAL GEOMETRIC SOLIDS. To the five symmetrical solids of the ancients is added the sphere (1), the most perfect of all created forms. The five Pythagorean solids are: the tetrahedron (2) with four equilateral triangles as faces; the cube (3) with six squares as faces; the octahedron (4) with eight equilateral triangles as faces; the

One of them, veiled with the white robes of the temple, urged the neophyte to enter into the halls of learning; the other, bedecked with jewels, symbolizing earthly treasures, and bearing in her hands a tray loaded with grapes (emblematic of false light), sought to lure him into the chambers of dissipation. This symbol is still preserved among the Tarot cards, where it is called The Forking of the Ways. The forked stick has been the symbol of life among many nations, and it was placed in the desert to indicate the presence of water.

Concerning the theory of transmigration as disseminated by Pythagoras, there are differences of opinion. According to one view, he taught that mortals who during their earthly existence had by their actions become like certain animals, returned to earth again in the form of the beasts which they had grown to resemble. Thus, a timid person would return in the form of a rabbit or a deer; a cruel person in the form of a wolf or other ferocious animal; and a cunning person in the guise of a fox. This concept, however, does not fit into the general Pythagorean scheme, and it is far more likely that it was given in an allegorical rather than a literal sense. It was intended to convey the idea that human beings become bestial when they allow themselves to be dominated by their own lower desires and destructive tendencies. It is probable that the term *transmigration* is to be understood as what is more commonly called *reincarnation,* a doctrine which Pythagoras must have contacted directly or indirectly in India and Egypt.

---

icosahedron (5) with twenty equilateral triangles as faces; and the dodecahedron (6) with twelve regular pentagons as faces.

The fact that Pythagoras accepted the theory of successive reappearances of the spiritual nature in human form is found in a footnote to Levi's *History of Magic:* "He was an important champion of what used to be called the doctrine of metempsychosis, understood as the soul's transmigration into successive bodies. He himself had been (a) Aethalides, a son of Mercury; (b) Euphorbus, son of Panthus, who perished at the hands of Menelaus in the Trojan war; (c) Hermotimus, a prophet of Clazomenae, a city of Ionia; (d) a humble fisherman; and finally (e) the philosopher of Samos."

Pythagoras also taught that each species of creatures had what he termed a seal, given to it by God, and that the physical form of each was the impression of this seal upon the wax of physical substance. Thus each body was stamped with the dignity of its divinely given pattern. Pythagoras believed that ultimately man would reach a state where he would cast off his gross nature and function in a body of spiritualized ether which would be in juxtaposition to his physical form at all times and which might be the eighth sphere, or Antichthon. From this he would ascend into the realm of the immortals, where by divine birthright he belonged.

Pythagoras taught that everything in nature was divisible into three parts and that no one could become truly wise who did not view every problem as being diagrammatically triangular. He said, "Establish the triangle and the problem is two-thirds solved"; further, "All things consist of three." In conformity with this viewpoint, Pythagoras divided the universe into three parts, which he called the *Supreme World,* the *Superior World,* and the *Inferior World.* The highest, or Supreme

World, was a subtle, interpenetrative spiritual essence pervading all things and therefore the true plane of the Supreme Deity itself, the Deity being in every sense omnipresent, omniactive, omnipotent, and omniscient. Both of the lower worlds existed within the nature of this supreme sphere.

The Superior World was the home of the immortals. It was also the dwelling place of the archetypes, or the seals; their natures in no manner partook of the material of earthiness, but they, casting their shadows upon the deep (the Inferior World), were cognizable only through their shadows. The third, or Inferior World, was the home of those creatures who partook of material substance or were engaged in labor with or upon material substance. Hence, this sphere was the home of the mortal gods, the Demiurgi, the angels who labor with men; also the dæmons who partake of the nature of the earth; and finally mankind and the lower kingdoms, those temporarily of the earth but capable of rising above that sphere by reason and philosophy.

The digits 1 and 2 are not considered numbers by the Pythagoreans, because they typify the two supermundane spheres. The Pythagorean numbers, therefore, begin with 3, the triangle, and 4, the square. These added to the 1 and the 2, produce the 10, the great number of all things, the archetype of the universe. The three worlds were called *receptacles*. The first was the receptacle of principles, the second was the receptacle of intelligences, and the third, or lowest, was the receptacle of quantities.

"The symmetrical solids were regarded by Pythagoras, and by the Greek thinkers after him, as of the greatest importance. To be perfectly symmetrical or regular, a solid must have an equal number of faces meeting at each of its angles, and these faces must be equal regular polygons, i. e., figures whose sides and angles are all equal. Pythagoras, perhaps, may be credited with the great discovery that there are only five such solids. . .

"Now, the Greeks believed the world (the material universe) to be composed of four elements-- earth, air, fire, water--and to the Greek mind the conclusion was inevitable that the shapes of the particles of the elements were those of the regular solids. Earth-particles were cubical, the cube being the regular solid possessed of greatest stability; fire- particles were tetrahedral, the tetrahedron being the simplest and, hence, lightest solid. Water-particles were icosahedral for exactly the reverse reason, whilst air-particles, as intermediate between the two latter, were octahedral. The dodecahedron was, to these ancient mathematicians, the most mysterious of the solids; it was by far the most difficult to construct, the accurate drawing of the regular pentagon necessitating a rather elaborate application of Pythagoras' great theorem. Hence the conclusion, as Plato put it, that 'this (the regular dodecahedron) the Deity employed in tracing the plan of the Universe. " (H. Stanley Redgrove, in *Bygone Beliefs.)*

Mr. Redgrove has not mentioned the fifth element of the ancient Mysteries, that which would make the analogy between the symmetrical solids and the elements complete. This fifth element, or ether, was called by the Hindus *akasa*. It was closely correlated with the hypothetical ether of modern science, and was the interpenetrative substance permeating all of the other elements and acting as a common solvent and common denominator of them. The twelve-faced solid also subtly referred to the Twelve Immortals who surfaced the universe, and also to the twelve convolutions of the human brain--the vehicles of those Immortals in the nature of man.

While Pythagoras, in accordance with others of his day, practiced divination (possibly arithmomancy), there is no accurate information concerning the methods which he used. He is believed to have had a remarkable wheel by means of which he could predict future events, and to have learned hydromancy from the Egyptians. He believed that brass had oracular powers, because even when everything was perfectly still there was always a rumbling sound in brass bowls. He once addressed a prayer to the spirit of a river and out of the water arose a voice, "Pythagoras, I greet thee." It is claimed for him that he was able to cause dæmons to enter into water and disturb its surface, and by means of the agitations certain things were predicted.

After having drunk from a certain spring one day, one of the Masters of Pythagoras announced that the spirit of the water had just predicted that a great earthquake would occur the next day--a prophecy which was fulfilled. It is highly probable that Pythagoras possessed hypnotic power, not only over man but also over animals. He caused a bird to change the course of its flight, a bear to cease its ravages upon a community, and a bull to change its diet, by the exercise of mental influence. He was also gifted with second sight, being able to see things at a distance and accurately describe incidents that had not yet come to pass.

PART III:

THE SYMBOLIC APHORISMS OF PYTHAGORAS

Iamblichus gathered thirty-nine of the symbolic sayings of Pythagoras and interpreted them. These have been translated from the Greek by Thomas Taylor. Aphorismic statement was one of the favorite methods of instruction used in the Pythagorean university of Crotona. Ten of the most representative of these aphorisms are reproduced below with a brief elucidation of their concealed meanings.

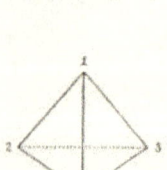

[3] I. *Declining from the public ways, walk in unfrequented paths.* By this it is to be understood that those who desire wisdom must seek it in solitude.

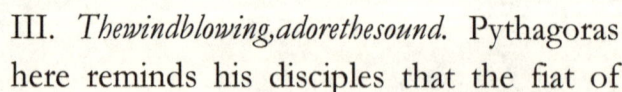

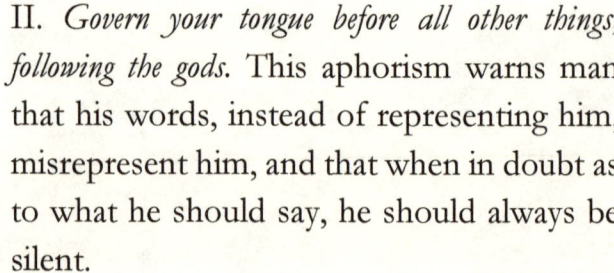

II. *Govern your tongue before all other things, following the gods.* This aphorism warns man that his words, instead of representing him, misrepresent him, and that when in doubt as to what he should say, he should always be silent.

III. *Thewindblowing,adorethesound.* Pythagoras here reminds his disciples that the fiat of

---

[3] Depiction of NUMBER RELATED TO FORM. Pythagoras taught that the dot symbolized the power of the number 1, the line the power of the number 2, the surface the power of the number 3, and the solid the power of the number 4.

God is heard in the voice of the elements, and that all things in Nature manifest through harmony, rhythm, order, or procedure the attributes of the Deity.

IV. *Assist a man in raising a burden; but do not assist him in laying it down.* The student is instructed to aid the diligent but never to assist those who seek to evade their responsibilities, for it is a great sin to encourage indolence.

V. *Speak not about Pythagoric concerns without light.* The world is herein warned that it should not attempt to interpret the mysteries of God and the secrets of the sciences without spiritual and intellectual illumination.

VI. *Having departed from your house, turn not back, for the furies will be your attendants.* Pythagoras here warns his followers that any who begin the search for truth and, after having learned part of the mystery, become discouraged and attempt to return again to their former ways of vice and ignorance, will suffer exceedingly; for it is better to know nothing about Divinity than to learn a little and then stop without learning all.

VII. *Nourish a cock, but sacrifice it not; for it is sacred to the sun and moon.* Two great lessons are concealed in this aphorism. The first is a warning against the sacrifice of living things to the gods, because life is sacred and man should not destroy it even as an offering to the Deity. The second warns man that the human body here referred to as a cock is sacred to the sun (God) and the moon (Nature), and should be guarded and preserved as man's most precious medium of expression. Pythagoras also warned his disciples against suicide.

VIII. *Receive not a swallow into your house.* This warns the seeker after truth not to allow drifting thoughts to come into his mind nor shiftless persons to enter into his life. He must ever surround himself with rationally inspired thinkers and with conscientious workers.

IX. *Offer not your right hand easily to anyone.* This warns the disciple to keep his own counsel and not offer wisdom and knowledge (his right hand) to such as are incapable of appreciating them. The hand here represents Truth, which raises those who have fallen because of ignorance; but as many of the unregenerate do not desire wisdom they will cut off the hand that is extended in kindness to them. Time alone can effect the redemption of the ignorant masses

X. When *rising from the bedclothes, roll them together, and obliterate the impression of the body.* Pythagoras directed his disciples who had awakened from the sleep of ignorance into the waking state of intelligence to eliminate from their recollection all memory of their former spiritual darkness; for a wise man in passing leaves no form behind him which others less intelligent, seeing, shall use as a mold for the casting of idols.

The most famous of the Pythagorean fragments are the *Golden Verses,* ascribed to Pythagoras himself, but concerning whose authorship there is an element of doubt. The *Golden Verses* contain a brief summary of the entire system of philosophy forming the basis of the educational doctrines of Crotona, or, as it is more commonly known, the Italic School.

These verses open by counseling the reader to love God, venerate the great heroes, and respect the dæmons and elemental inhabitants. They then urge man to think carefully and industriously concerning his daily life, and to prefer the treasures of the mind and soul to accumulations of earthly goods. The verses also promise man that if he will rise above his lower material nature and cultivate self-control, he will ultimately be acceptable in the sight of the gods, be reunited with them, and partake of their immortality. (It is rather significant to note that Plato paid a great price for some of the manuscripts of Pythagoras which had been saved from the destruction of Crotona. See *Historia Deorum Fatidicorum*, Geneva, 1675.)

PART IV:

PYTHAGOREAN ASTRONOMY

According to Pythagoras, the position of each body in the universe was determined by the essential dignity of that body. The popular concept of his day was that the earth occupied the center of the solar system; that the planets, including the sun and moon, moved about the earth; and that the earth itself was flat and square. Contrary to this concept, and regardless of criticism, Pythagoras declared that fire was the most important of all the elements; that the center was the most important part of every body; and that, just as Vesta's fire was in the midst of every home, so in the midst of the universe was a flaming sphere of celestial radiance. This central globe he called the *Tower of Jupiter*, the *Globe of Unity*, the *Grand Monad*, and the *Altar of Vesta*. As the sacred number 10 symbolized the sum of all parts and the completeness of all things, it was only natural for Pythagoras to divide the universe into ten spheres, symbolized by ten concentric circles. These circles began at the center with the globe of Divine Fire; then came the seven planers, the earth, and another mysterious planet, called *Antichthon*, which was never visible.

Opinions differ as to the nature of *Antichthon*. Clement of Alexandria believed that it represented the mass of the heavens; others held the opinion that it was the moon. More probably it was the mysterious eighth sphere of the ancients, the dark planet which moved in the same orbit as the earth but which was always concealed from the earth by the body of the sun, being in exact opposition to the earth at all times. Is this the mysterious Lilith concerning which astrologers have speculated so long?

Isaac Myer has stated: "The Pythagoreans held that each star was a world having its own atmosphere, with an immense extent surrounding it, of aether." (See *The Qabbalah.*) The disciples of Pythagoras also highly revered the planet Venus, because it was the only planet bright enough to cast a shadow. As the morning star, Venus is visible before sunrise, and as the evening star it shines forth immediately after sunset. Because of these qualities, a number of names have been given to it by the ancients. Being visible in the sky at sunset, it was called *vesper,* and as it arose before the sun, it was called *the false light, the star of the morning,* or *Lucifer,* which means *the light- bearer.* Because of this relation to the sun, the planet was also referred to as Venus, Astarte, Aphrodite, Isis, and The Mother of the Gods. It is possible that: at some seasons of the year in certain latitudes the fact that Venus was a crescent could be detected without the aid of a telescope. This would account for the crescent which is often seen in connection with the goddesses of antiquity, the stories of which do not agree with the phases of the moon. The accurate knowledge which Pythagoras possessed concerning astronomy he undoubtedly secured in the Egyptian temples, for their priests understood the true relationship of the heavenly bodies many thousands of years before that knowledge was revealed to the uninitiated world. The fact that the knowledge he acquired in the temples enabled him to make assertions requiring two thousand years to check proves why Plato and Aristotle so highly esteemed the profundity of the ancient Mysteries. In the midst of comparative scientific ignorance, and without the aid of any modern instruments, the priest-philosophers had discovered the true fundamentals of universal dynamics.

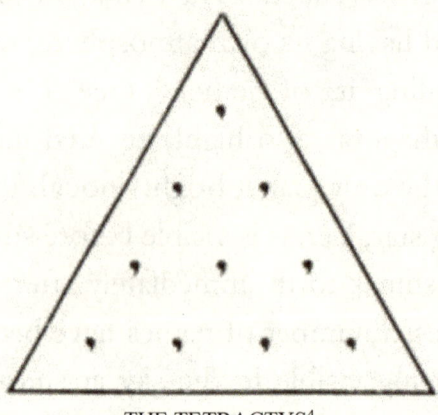

THE TETRACTYS[4]

An interesting application of the Pythagorean doctrine of geometric solids as expounded by Plato is found in *The Canon*. "Nearly all the old philosophers," says its anonymous author, "devised an harmonic theory with respect to the universe, and the practice continued till the old mode of philosophizing died out. Kepler (1596), in order to demonstrate the Platonic doctrine, that the universe was formed of the five regular solids, proposed the following rule. 'The earth is a circle, the measurer of all. Round it describe a dodecahedron; the circle inclosing this will be Mars. Round Mars describe a tetrahedron; the sphere inclosing this will be Jupiter. Describe a cube round Jupiter; the sphere containing this will be Saturn.

---

[4] Theon of Smyrna declares that the ten dots, or tetractys of Pythagoras, was a symbol of the greatest importance, for to the discerning mind it revealed the mystery of universal nature. The Pythagoreans bound themselves by the following oath: "By Him who gave to our soul the tetractys, which hath the fountain and root of ever-springing nature."

Now inscribe in the earth an icosahedron; the circle inscribed in it will be Venus. Inscribe an octahedron in Venus; the circle inscribed in it will be Mercury' (Mysterium *Cosmographicum*, 1596). This rule cannot be taken seriously as a real statement of the proportions of the cosmos, fox it bears no real resemblance to the ratios published by Copernicus in the beginning of the sixteenth century. Yet Kepler was very proud of his formula, and said he valued it more than the Electorate of Saxony. It was

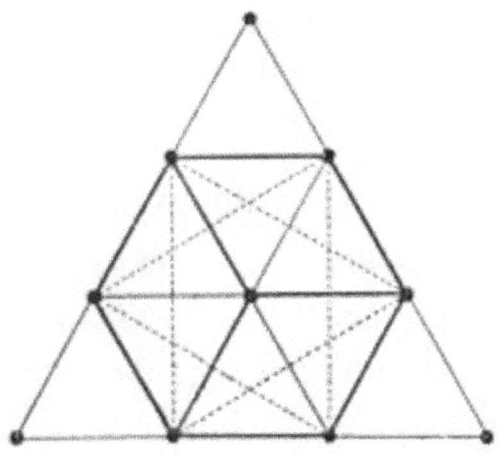

THE CUBE AND THE STAR[5]

also approved by those two eminent authorities, Tycho and Galileo, who evidently understood it. Kepler himself never gives the least hint of how his precious rule is to be interpreted." Platonic astronomy was not concerned with the

---

[5] By connecting the ten dots of the tetractys, nine triangles are formed. Six of these are involved in the forming of the cube. The same triangles, when lines are properly drawn between them, also reveal the six-pointed star with a dot in the center. Only seven dots are used in forming the cube and the star. Qabbalistically, the three unused corner dots represent the threefold, invisible causal nature of the universe, while the seven dots involved in the cube and the star are the Elohim--the Spirits of the seven creative periods. The Sabbath, or seventh day, is the central dot.

material constitution or arrangement of the heavenly bodies, but considered the stars and planers primarily as focal points of Divine intelligence. Physical astronomy was regarded as the science of "shadows," philosophical astronomy the science of "realities."

www.ingramcontent.com/pod-product-compliance
Lightning Source LLC
LaVergne TN
LVHW041459070426
835507LV00009B/687